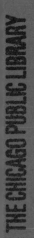

Smokejumpers

ELAINE LANDAU
PHOTOGRAPHS BY BEN KLAFFKE

The Millbrook Press   Brookfield, Connecticut

For Sarah Sutin.
E.L.

For the brave smokejumpers of California and
of McCall Smokejumper Base in Idaho.
B.K.

Photographs on pages 4 and 16–17 courtesy
of Smokejumper Peter Bryant.

Library of Congress Cataloging-in-Publication Data
Landau, Elaine.
Smokejumpers / Elaine Landau / photographs by Ben Klaffke.
p. cm.
ISBN 0-7613-2324-4 (lib. bdg.)
1. Smokejumpers—Juvenile literature. 2. Wildfire fighters—Juvenile literature.
[1. Smokejumpers. 2. Wildfire fighters. 3. Firefighters.
4. Occupations.] I. Klaffke, Ben, ill. II. Title.
SD421.23 .L36 2002
634.9'618—dc21 2001030974

Published by The Millbrook Press, Inc.
2 Old New Milford Road
Brookfield, Connecticut 06804
www.millbrookpress.com

The author, photographer, and publisher would like to thank
Mike Apicello, public-affairs officer at the National Interagency Fire
Center, and Arlen P. Cravens, base manager of the Region Five
Smokejumpers of the USDA Forest Service, Pacific Southwest
Region, for their valuable input.

During a typical fire season there are about 100,000 wild-land fires throughout the United States.

Alarge forest fire is spreading rapidly. Tall, stately trees turn into flaming torches. Dry grass and brush light up like matches. The heat is intense. You cannot see the sky—it is hidden by a cloud of smoke. More and more ground is taken by the advancing flames. Now a whole forest is at risk, as well as homes and even communities.

This is not an uncommon occurrence. In many areas of the United States the warmer months are also the *fire season*. The fire season in the West, for example, runs from about June 1 to October 15 of each year. Weeks of hot, dry weather during this time make conditions ripe for wildfires. Often these blazes are sparked by *dry lightning storms*. In these storms, lightning strikes without rain. It creates a spark that ignites the parched forest region. At other times, careless campers are to blame. Either way, the wind frequently drives flames through densely wooded areas known as *wildlands*.

Under the worst conditions, high, gusty winds can cause a number of fires to burn into one another. The result can be swiftly growing wildfires that destroy everything in their path. National forests, as well as vast areas of grass-land and prairie, are turned into flaming infernos.

From the time they arrive at the scene of a fire . . .

The Smokejumper Base at McCall, Idaho

Highly skilled troops of able-bodied men and women are called in to battle this brutal and frequently devastating foe. Some *crews* are trained to speedily arrive at remote wildlands, where wildfires often start. They are airborne firefighters who parachute to the scene from airplanes. Their specialty is fighting wildfires in places that other firefighters cannot easily get to—areas with no highways or even roads. These daring and determined people are known as *smokejumpers*.

Today there are about four hundred smoke-jumpers in the United States. They work out of nine bases in Idaho, Alaska, Montana, Oregon, California, Wyoming, and Washington. However, they can be sent anywhere at a moment's notice. Smokejumpers protect millions of acres of wilderness and remote territory. This includes national forests, grasslands, state forests, and privately owned wooded areas. For more than sixty years they have parachuted from the sky to fight wildland fires.

. . . to when they determine that the blaze is under control, a smokejumper's job is both exciting and dangerous.

To Be a Smokejumper

If you think anyone can be a smokejumper, think again. Each year hundreds of well-qualified people apply for the job. Yet, depending on the need, only between twenty and sixty individuals will usually be chosen.

Smokejumping is a physically demanding job. All smokejumpers have to be physically fit.

Smokejumpers have to be in peak physical condition. Battling a spreading wilderness fire may involve life-threatening risks. There are many physical hazards that can take an especially hard toll on the body.

A sudden wind shift can unexpectedly land a parachuting smokejumper on hard or rocky *terrain*. Sometimes the smokejumper may be knocked unconscious or suffer broken bones. Moving rapidly through steep and densely forested mountainous areas can result in serious cuts, bruises, and other injuries. Smokejumpers also often have to deal with long periods of exposure to heat and smoke while having limited supplies, including food and water.

It is crucial that smokejumpers remain physically fit and mentally alert. They must be able to work under pressure. All smokejumper crew members must be able to do what is expected of them. The team's effectiveness at battling the fire is at stake. So is the safety of the crew as a whole.

Smokejumper rookies arrive at the base filled with energy and hope. They will be spending a lot of time there in the weeks ahead. All recruits must pass a challenging physical endurance test. They are required to do seven chin-ups, forty-five sit-ups, and twenty-five push-ups. They also have to run 1.5 miles (2.4 kilometers) in less than eleven minutes. The entire test must be taken at one time, with only a five-minute break between the various exercises.

Those who pass go on to the next step. These rookies start a training program that teaches them the smokejumpers' special approach to wildland firefighting. The training lasts about six weeks. During that time the rookies are tested on each skill taught. Those who don't measure up are not selected to be smokejumpers.

Training begins in a classroom. Smokejumper trainees have an opportunity to ask questions and fully understand different aspects of wilderness firefighting before any actual "hands-on" training begins. From the classroom, they go

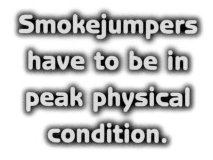

Smokejumpers have to be in peak physical condition.

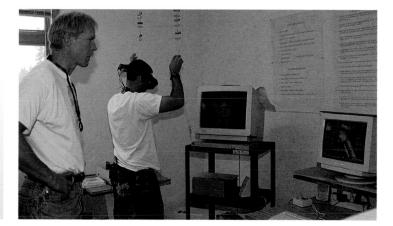

Some smokejumper training involves the latest technology. This smokejumper is using a virtual reality device that helps train for a very important aspect of his job: jumping out of an airplane.

Training on a jump tower

on to aerial firefighting and parachute jumping. The trainees learn aircraft procedures, how to exit a plane, and how to use a parachute. They learn what to do if the parachute becomes caught in a tree or if they land in water.

Smokejumpers will tell you that parachuting is an essential part of their training. Before jumping from a plane they practice jumping from *jump towers* that are about 50 feet (15 meters) off the ground. This helps them get used to the feeling of falling through the air. There are fifteen training jumps, ranging from simple landings to parachuting into more difficult terrain. Rookies must learn to perform the jumps flawlessly, and they are continually evaluated.

Smokejumper training also includes climbing trees with tree-climbing spurs and harness ropes. This climbing gear allows the smokejumpers on the job to speedily retrieve parachutes and supplies dropped from planes that might land there. In addition, smokejumper trainees practice cutting down trees with chain saws as well as using a compass and map in the woods.

When fighting fires, smokejumpers often have to carry large amounts of gear and equipment for long distances. Recruits also prepare for this during the training program. Before being sent into the field, trainees have to haul gear and equipment weighing 110 pounds (50 kilograms) for at least 3 miles (5 kilometers). They must complete this exercise in less than an hour and a half.

New recruits are not the only ones who train at the smokejumper base. Experienced smokejumpers take refresher courses there, too. Some receive

Emergency Medical Technician (EMT) training. This prepares them to handle crew emergencies in the field. Fighting wilderness fires is difficult and dangerous work. There are bound to be injuries.

They also learn the newest wilderness firefighting techniques. This is especially important. Today, forest ecologists believe that not all forest fires should be fought. Fire is part of the natural growth cycle of certain types of forests. Extinguishing small forest fires can lead to overcrowded forests. Forests filled with *vegetation* tend to burn hotter, creating more intense fires. If nature were left to take its course, small fires would regularly clear wooded areas of dead trees, leaves, and shrubs—the fuel that feeds raging blazes.

That is why smokejumpers at times serve more as fire managers than firefighters. They may allow a fire to partly burn without letting things get out of hand. However, in many cases, fires cannot be left to burn. Increasing numbers of people have moved closer to national forests and other wooded

Today, forest ecologists believe that not all forest fires should be fought.

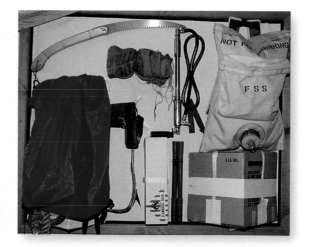

All smokejumpers have to carry the equipment they will use to fight a fire. Pictured is some of the equipment that is carried in a smokejumper's pack.

15

lands. Their lives and property would be at risk if smokejumpers and other wildland firefighters did not put out fires that come dangerously close to homes and communities.

These firefighters take their work seriously. However, most work as smokejumpers only during fire season. The rest of the year they may be teachers, loggers, or mechanics. Some smokejumpers are painters, students, racecar drivers, or writers. A few smokejumpers have even been artists and lawyers. One smokejumper was an astronaut. But regardless of what they do the rest of the year, many return each summer to fight fires.

Fires are a necessary part of the natural cycle of a forest. That is why smokejumpers sometimes serve more as fire *managers* than fire *fighters*.

From packing gear to doing paperwork, there is always plenty to keep smokejumpers busy between fire calls or during the off season.

A small number of smokejumpers stay at the base year-round. Most of these train other wildland firefighters and prepare smokejumper equipment for the next fire season. Some also do paperwork or help with various forestry projects. All smokejumpers work for the United States government.

During the fire season, smokejumpers spend much of their time away from their bases and homes. They may be called to battle blazes in numerous parts of the western United States and Alaska. But while waiting at the base, they are always busy. Besides following a daily fitness routine, they repair firefighting equipment and practice their smokejumper skills.

Some smokejumpers are specially trained in parachute packing or rigging. This is done in a separate area of the smokejumper base known as the *loft*.

Keeping fit is another way smokejumpers keep busy.

Repairing...

...and rigging parachutes are important tasks that require much skill and an eye for detail.

There, smokejumpers inspect and fold the parachutes on long tables. They carefully check them for twists, tangles, and twigs. When necessary, these smokejumper riggers also repair parachutes. They sew up holes and fix damaged lines. Well aware that a malfunctioning parachute could result in a crew member's injury or death, they pay close attention to details when doing this work. Their efforts have paid off. There have been very few serious parachute malfunctions in the history of smokejumping.

All the training and work that smokejumpers do prepares them for their actual firefighting assignments. It is then that their skills are put to the test.

Fire Call

A fire call comes into the dispatcher's office at a smokejumper base. A wildfire has been spotted. Seconds later the base springs into action.

A siren goes off, alerting the smokejumpers on duty. A smokejumper supervisor known as a *spotter* immediately plots the fire's location on a map. It is important to know exactly where the blaze has begun.

When a fire call comes into the smokejumper base, spotters plot the fire's location on a map.

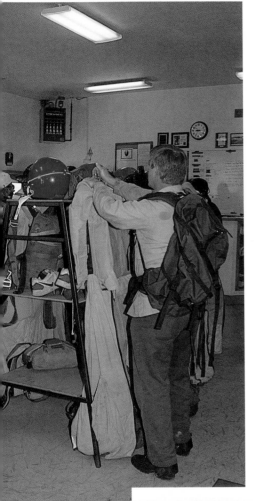

Smokejumpers gear up for a fire.

Meanwhile, the smokejumpers start to suit up. Their outfits and equipment have been readied for use. First the smokejumpers put on a fire-resistant bright yellow shirt and green pants. When in the field, the shirt's color helps them to be seen through the smoke and debris.

Over the shirt and pants goes a yellow jumpsuit made of fire-resistant material. The jumpsuit is worn while parachuting to the ground. It protects the wearer from sharp tree twigs, branches, and rocks. The jumpsuit is heavily padded in the shoulders, elbows, back, ribs, hips, and knees. This provides cushioning for hard landings. During the jump, smokejumpers also wear a motorcycle helmet equipped with a wire face mask for added protection.

The smokejumper's parachute harness then goes on over the jumpsuit. It contains two parachutes. The main parachute is worn over the back. An emergency reserve parachute is worn across the chest. Smokejumpers also carry a gear bag in which a hard hat, work gloves, *fire shelter*, compass, and other essential items have been packed. When smokejumpers exit the aircraft the combined weight of their suit and gear is about 80 pounds (36 kilograms).

As the smokejumpers dress, they can hear the roar of the aircraft starting up on the runway outside. After the smokejumpers quickly board, the plane takes off, heading for the fire zone. On arrival, the firefighters do not immediately parachute out of the plane.

First, the spotter along with the *crew leader* (also known as the *crew boss*) must determine the best way to attack the blaze. They develop a strategy as the plane circles the fire area, offering them an overhead view of the situation. The smokejumpers on the aircraft also look out the windows. Surveying the fire from above helps them pick up important details that may later be useful on the ground. But until they land, the smokejumpers can never be quite sure of what awaits them.

The spotter and crew leader decide how many of the smokejumpers aboard will be needed. If the fire has just begun, as few as two firefighters

On board the aircraft, smokejumpers wait for word from their crew leader about the strategy they will use to bring the fire under control.

can handle things. In other cases, ten times as many smokejumpers are necessary. A *jump spot* must also be selected. This is the site where the smokejumpers will land.

Once an exact jump spot is picked, the plane slows down to circle the area. The spotter tosses weighted paper streamers out of the aircraft. This is done to learn the wind's speed and direction over the jump spot. If the streamers land on the jump spot, the parachuters probably will, too.

The aircraft continues to circle between 1,500 and 3,000 feet (457 and 914 meters) above the jump spot. On each pass around the spot, one to three smokejumpers exit the plane. If more were to go at the same time, some would miss the jump spot, and that could be dangerous.

While in the aircraft, the spotter and crew leader use their radios to remain in touch with the dispatcher. This is crucial in case additional help or supplies are needed. On the ground the smokejumpers will also use radios to keep in touch with their crew leader and one another. In an emergency, a smoke-jumper's radio can be a lifesaving tool.

Radios are only a small part of the equipment these fire-fighters rely on. Once they have landed at a jump site, they gather together all the necessary items. These are dropped to them from the aircraft after all the smokejumpers are safely on the ground.

In making the drop, the aircraft comes in low—its altitude will be only about 200 feet (60 meters) above the trees. It may seem as if the pilot is about to crash into the forest, but that does not happen. Instead, tools and supplies are dropped from the aircraft by cargo parachutes. These

A smokejumper demonstrates the proper way to prepare to exit the aircraft while the spotter looks on.

Once the firepacks have landed, their parachutes are removed and the smoke-jumpers unpack them. Pictured are some of the supplies that are dropped to the smoke-jumpers at the scene of a fire.

firepacks, as they are called, contain hand tools such as shovels, along with sleeping bags and enough food and water for two days.

Depending on the nature and extent of the fire, more supplies may be needed. Therefore chain saws, backpack pumps, tree-climbing spurs, and additional firefighting instruments can be dropped as well.

Once on the ground, the smokejumper crew leader determines if there are enough people and supplies to do the job. As soon as the leader is certain that they are in good shape, the aircraft leaves. The smokejumper crew can contact the dispatcher by radio, but other than that they are now on their own.

The smokejumpers then prepare to face the fire. The crew leader lays out a specific plan for their attack. One important rule they follow is safety first. Before the crew begins its work, the crew leader identifies a safety zone. The safety zone is an area that the smokejumpers can quickly go to if the fire gets out of hand and they find that their lives are at risk. This can easily happen

On the ground, the crew leader briefs the smokejumpers and makes sure they all know how to get to the area that has been chosen as the safety zone.

in the course of fighting a wildfire. Depending on wind shifts, weather conditions, and the terrain, wildfires can act unpredictably.

One important rule is safety first

After a safety zone has been determined, the crew leader makes sure that each smokejumper knows where it is and the various routes to it. Having more than one escape route is essential since any route can suddenly become blocked by a spreading fire. Strategically located *lookouts* alert the smokejumpers to changes in the fire's direction. They radio the smokejumpers when it is time to head for the safety zone.

If the smokejumpers should suddenly become trapped by the fire, they use the fire shelters packed in their gear bags. A fire shelter is a lifesaving tent made of shiny, silver fire-resistant material that a firefighter can crawl into when surrounded by flames.

A smokejumper's fire shelter looks like nothing more than a tent made from aluminum foil, but it's actually a very effective tool to use in case of emergency.

The smokejumpers quickly set up their individual fire shelters in a cleared area. In the shelters, they lie on their stomachs with their feet and hands in straps at each of the structure's four corners. The shelter traps a pocket of cooler air for the person to breathe. This protects the firefighter's lungs and airways. The smokejumpers remain in the shelters until the crew leader indicates that it is safe to leave. A smokejumper is never without a fire shelter. It is hoped that these lifesaving devices will not often be necessary.

The first step in controlling a wildfire is to rob it of the forest growth it needs to continue spreading. To do this, the smokejumpers build a *fireline*. A fireline is a wide strip of cleared land encircling the blaze. In creating a fireline, the firefighters remove all the trees, logs, brush, and dry leaves within the strip. The size of the fireline depends on how intense the fire is. Many firelines are just 2 feet (60 centimeters) wide, while others may be 200 feet (60 meters) wide. Firelines are crucial in containing wildfires. Deprived of the fuel it needs to burn, the fire cannot advance.

This picture of a fireline was taken after the blaze was out.

Securing a fireline is not an easy task. It takes a lot of hard work. The smokejumpers must use their chain saws and crosscut saws to bring down burning trees. *Fire shovels*, which have a tapered blade and sharpened edges, are especially helpful in the process. They are designed for scraping and digging in forests. A special ax known as a *Pulaski* is used to help clear the fireline.

In some cases firefighters also need to set *backfires*. These are fires purposely lit along the inner edge of a fireline. Backfires are used to burn the timber in the space between the fireline and the advancing fire. The idea behind this measure is to deprive the blaze of any additional fuel in its path. Smokejumpers use *drip torches* to light backfires. These torches squirt small streams of fire.

Wilderness firefighting is exhausting. Fourteen- to eighteen-hour days of grueling work in burning forests are not uncommon for smokejumpers. Unfortunately, at times their efforts are hampered by the wind. Pieces of burning forest debris can easily be blown past firelines and into formerly safe areas.

In heavily wooded regions, new blazes known as *spot fires* can quickly begin this way. Once the fireline has been constructed, smokejumpers routinely check the area for any fires caused by windblown material. Ideally, these small spot fires will be swiftly put out before they can spread.

Some of the equipment smoke-jumpers use, including fire shovels, Pulaskis, and a drip torch (far left).

When dealing with large fires, however, smokejumpers frequently rely on help from the sky. In these cases air tankers arrive on the scene. These are aircraft used to carry and drop a water-based fire-retardant mixture that works to stop the flames.

The fire retardant coats the forest growth with a sticky substance that cools it and makes it less likely to burn. An air tanker can carry up to 3,000 gallons (11,356 liters) of fire retardant. But often that is just the first step of the air attack. After the retardant is dropped, helicopters may be used to drop water directly on the blaze and on smoldering areas known as hot spots. The water is carried in huge buckets that swing beneath the aircraft.

A helicopter drops water on a fire's hot spot.

On the ground, smokejumpers have marked this hot spot for a helicopter to drop water on.

A smokejumper uses his backpack pump to extinguish a smoldering area.

Although the smokejumpers have done a great deal to contain the fire, the situation is still too uncertain for them to rest. Once a firm fireline has been established and things appear to be largely under control, they begin the *mop-up* phase of the operation.

During mop-up, the smokejumpers make certain that the fire is fully extinguished. Using their backpack pumps, they put out any remaining burning material near the fireline. Smoldering embers are extinguished with damp soil. The smokejumpers also cut down *snags*. These are standing dead trees or parts of dead trees.

Only after all this is done can the smokejumper crew get a sorely needed break from firefighting. They eat the prepared food they brought with them. After that the crew members take out their sleeping bags for a few hours of rest.

When they awake they check to make sure that the fire is completely out. This is done by crawling along the forest floor to feel for any hot spots with their bare hands. Every inch of ground in the burn area is examined. This process is known as *cold trailing*. Once the entire fire zone is cool, the fire is considered out. The smokejumpers can then head back to the base.

Cold trailing is the final step in making sure a forest fire is fully extinguished.

The smokejumper crew leader radios the dispatcher to arrange for transportation back. Sometimes a mule train can be sent in to haul out the gear and tools. But more often than not the smokejumpers pack up their own equipment and walk to the nearest path, road, or helicopter pickup point. It is not unusual for them to travel more than 5 miles (8 kilometers) on foot while carrying *pack-out bags* (backpacks) that weigh as much as 115 pounds (52 kilograms).

With his pack-out bag, this smoke-jumper heads on foot to the pickup point, which may be close to ten miles (sixteen kilometers) away.

Scorched and burned hills and flatlands are the results of a wildland fire near Paskenta, in northern California. During fire season, smokejumpers will be called to many blazes in areas like this.

Even after the smokejumpers return to the base, they usually do not have much time to rest. During the fire season, they may likely be called again soon. Smokejumpers often travel long distances to go where they are needed. Some of their most challenging firefighting assignments last for weeks.

For most smokejumpers, however, the hard work and danger are overshadowed by the importance of their work. Smokejumpers do more than control fires. They help preserve our forests. Sometimes they save lives and homes as well. Every time they leave for a fire, they are doing an important job for us all. Their bravery and value cannot be measured.

Another fire successfully battled . . .

Smokejumper Talk

AIR TANKER — A fixed-wing aircraft used to both carry and deliver *fire-retardant* solutions.

BACKFIRE — A fire set along the inside edge of a *fireline* to reduce a forest fire's fuel.

COLD TRAILING — The process by which smokejumpers make sure a fire is fully out by crawling along the forest floor to feel for any smoldering spots with their bare hands.

CREW — A group of smokejumpers under the direction of a person known as the *crew leader* or *crew boss*.

DRIP TORCH — A torch that drips a fiery combination of liquid diesel fuel and gasoline.

DRY LIGHTNING STORM — A thunderstorm in which there is lightning but no rain.

FIRELINE — A cleared area created by smokejumpers around a fire to rob the blaze of fuel.

FIREPACKS — Packages containing tools and equipment dropped to smokejumpers by cargo parachutes.

FIRE RETARDANT — A chemical substance that reduces the ability of forest fuel to burn.

FIRE SEASON — The time of year when wildfires are most likely to occur; from June to October in the western United States.

FIRE SHELTER — A flame-resistant shelter that can be quickly set up if a smokejumper becomes trapped by a fire.

FIRE SHOVEL — A shovel with a tapered blade and sharpened edges, ideal for digging and scraping in a forest.

HOT SPOT — A smoldering area.

JUMP SPOT — The site in the forest selected as a landing place for the smokejumpers.

JUMP TOWER — A tower that smokejumpers use for parachute training.

LOFT — A room at the smokejumper base where parachutes are inspected after every use.

LOOKOUTS — Strategically located people who watch fires and report on them to smokejumpers.

MOP-UP — The process of extinguishing or removing burning material near the *fireline*.

PACK-OUT BAG — A bag used by smokejumpers to carry gear and tools out of the forest after a fire has been extinguished.

PULASKI — A special ax used by smokejumpers to help clear wooded areas.

SMOKEJUMPERS — Firefighters who parachute to fires, often in remote areas where there are no highways or roads.

SNAG — A standing dead tree or part of a dead tree.

SPOT FIRE — A new blaze begun by burning windblown material.

SPOTTER — A smokejumper supervisor who plots the location of a fire on a map and helps select the jump site for the parachuters.

TERRAIN — A land area.

VEGETATION — Plant growth.

WILDLAND — An uninhabited, undeveloped area.

Fiery Books

Beil, Karen. *Fire in Their Eyes: Wildfires and the People Who Fight Them*. San Diego, CA: Harcourt Brace, 1999.

Cone, Patrick. *Wildfire*. Minneapolis: Carolrhoda Books, 1997.

Fortney, Mary T. *Fire Station Number 4: The Daily Life of Firefighters*. Minneapolis: Carolrhoda Books, 1998.

Kuklin, Susan. *Fighting Fires*. New York: Bradbury Press, 1993.

Masoff, Joy. *Fire*. New York: Scholastic, 1998.

Patent, Dorothy Hinshaw. *Fire: Friend or Foe*. New York: Clarion, 1998.

Pringle, Laurence. *Fire in the Forest: A Cycle of Growth and Renewal*. New York: Atheneum, 1995.

Royston, Angela. *Fire Fighters*. New York: DK Publishing, 1998.

Simon, Seymour. *Wildfires*. New York: Morrow, 1996.

Fiery Web Sites

www.smokejumpers.com
The official home of the National Smokejumper Association, this site contains smoke-jumper and wildfire news, a history of smokejumping, photo archives, and video clips.

www.fs.fed.us/fire/operations/jumpers/mccall
Get an in-depth look at the world of smokejumpers at the official Web site of the McCall smokejumper base.

www.smokeybear.com
Explore Smokey Bear's official home page for some forest and campfire fun.

www.sparky.org
Sparky the Fire Dog's official home page is an interactive site with fire prevention news, games, and other fun activities. Sparky is the official "spokesdog" for the National Fire Protection Association.

Index